D0559502

OTHER GIFTBOOKS IN THIS SERIES

baby boy!   *mum*   *happy day!*
baby girl!   *dad*   *hope! dream!*
friend   *daughter*   *smile*

Published simultaneously in 2007 by Helen Exley Giftbooks in Great Britain
and Helen Exley Giftbooks LLC in the USA.

12 11 10 9 8 7 6 5 4 3

Illustrations © Joanna Kidney 2007
Copyright © Helen Exley 2007
Text copyright – see page 94.
The moral right of the author has been asserted.

ISBN 13: 978-1-84634-008-6

Edited by Helen Exley
Pictures by Joanna Kidney
Printed in China

Helen Exley Giftbooks, 16 Chalk Hill, Watford, Herts WD19 4BG, UK.

www.helenexleygiftbooks.com

HELEN EXLEY

Sister

PICTURES BY JOANNA KIDNEY

Having a sister means having
one of the most beautiful and unique
of human relationships.
We share with our sisters
a special intimacy, a powerful communion
of heart and mind.

AUTHOR UNKNOWN

She is your witness,
who sees you at your worst and best,
and loves you anyway.
She is your partner in crime,
your midnight companion,
someone who knows
when you are smiling,
even in the dark.

BARBARA ALPERT

She is... my light, and my sunshir

y life would be dark without her.

MARY ABBAJAY

WHAT IS A SISTER?

Someone to confide in,
a girl that bosses you about,
a person that sides with you,
a friend for life, a younger mother,
someone who hogs the shower,
smells like a chemist's shop,
a person who is understanding,
That's a sister!!!

LOUISE DYE, AGE 11

A sister is your finest guide.
Escorting you along unfamiliar paths.
Supporting you
each time you stumble.
Encouraging you when the way is hard.
Congratulating you
when you reach your destination.
Always with you
wherever you choose to go.

STUART & LINDA MACFARLANE

A big part of paradise was caring
for my baby sister.... from day one,
Michie's been more
        than a sister to me.
She is one of my life's
        absolute treasures.

KATHIE LEE GIFFORD

The baby gazes enraptured at her sister,
watching her draw and write,
make faces, dance for her.
The six-year-old cradles her, kisses her,
winds the music box. Reads her stories,
delights in this new treasure.
Her own, her very own dear sister.

PAM BROWN, B.1928

To have a loving relationship
with a sister is not simply to have

uddy or confidante, it is
to have a soulmate for life.

VICTORIA SECUNDA

She never corrected me, she simply
supplied me with information regarding how
things could be conveniently done...
Now I had someone to walk with who
would pick me up if I fell
and would pluck me back if I started to cross
the road without making sure it was clear.

DAME REBECCA WEST (1892–1983),
ON HER SISTER WINIFRED

My mother told me that when
Rosey started school, I was so devastated
that I sat on the couch
looking out of the window,
waiting for her return.
There were days when
I sat like that for hours.

GERALDINE BARR, ON HER SISTER ROSEANNE

How do people get through life
if they have to go
to a playground
by themselves?

DONNA MASIEJCZYK, FROM "SISTERS"

When you changed her,
wiped her nose, mopped up her porridge
and picked up her toys,
a baby sister seems a pretty poor idea.
But then she grins her gummy grin
and offers you her soggy rusk
and gives you a sticky kiss.
And you love her forever and forever.

PAM BROWN, B.1928

She was my protector,
my lookout,
my voice at the drugstore counter
when I was too shy to ask for help.
She killed the spiders,
led the way home,
rang the doorbells for trick-or-treat.

LISA GRUNWALD, FROM "GLAMOUR",
JULY 1995

Sisters can be pets, or pet peeves.
However we may regard them,
either as our
mirror images or our opposites,
sisters are an important
part of our lives.

LOIS L. KAUFMAN

A sister is naggings and needlings,
whispers and whisperings.
Bribery. Thumpings.
Borrowings. Breakings.
Kisses and cuddlings.
Lendings. Surprises.
Defendings and comfortings.
Welcomings home.

PAM BROWN, B.1928

Sisters are
connected throughout their lives
by a special bond
– whether they like it or not.
For better or worse....

BRIGID MCCONVILLE,
FROM "SISTERS: LOVE AND CONFLICT
WITHIN THE LIFELONG BOND"

Your secrets are her secrets.
Her stockings are your stockings.
And you give and take
the sort of advice on clothes, cash,
spots and boyfriends that no other
member of the family would dare.

VICTORIA BARCLAY,
FROM "DAILY MAIL", AUGUST 4, 1987

Thank you for the times you let me

ry, very quietly in the early hours.

PAM BROWN, B.1928

The only person
I've ever been prepared to sing to,
and read the Three Bears
for the fifty-fifth time,
is my little sister.

PAM BROWN, B.1928

Everything glamorous,
comely, elegant, fragrant,
remote, feminine, and forbidden
was my sister Charlotte for me.

DORIS KEARNS GOODWIN, B.1943,
FROM "WAIT TILL NEXT YEAR"

How do people
make it through life without a sister?
I need her as much as she needs me.
She is my biggest security in life.
Mary creates for me a sense
of well-being beyond any relationship
I have ever experienced.

SARA CORPENING,
ABOUT HER TWIN SISTER MARY

Who else would endure
my sillier moods
or forgive my more idiotic mistakes?
Only you.
Why, I can't fathom.
But I give thanks that you do.

PAM BROWN, B.1928

We may be stars to the world,
but we are not stars to one another.
We are just sisters.

THE FAMOUS BEVERLEY SISTERS

My sister Gigi is
the first person I call with good news,
so we can celebrate together....
No matter what I'm feeling,
her response is the one
I want to hear before anyone else's.

KATHLEEN O'KEEFE

She has been the sun of my life,
the gilder of every pleasure,
    the soother of every sorrow,
I have not had a thought
        concealed from her....

CASSANDRA AUSTEN,
ABOUT HER SISTER JANE.

Sisters sometimes talk about
how they can see through each other,
never misled by the other's pretences,
instinctively knowing
the other's true feelings.

TARA WOODS

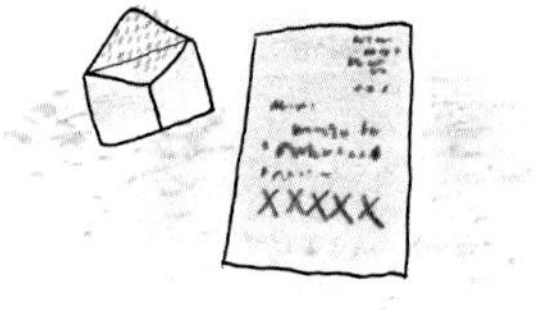
XXXXX

I always feel her presence
wherever I go and when I am having
new experiences, or meeting
new people, I feel she is always there
in me as a way of making sense
of the new experiences.
I'll think, "Oh Sonia would love this"
or I send her a letter.

MAYA RAVAL, B.1967

Rediscovering the fun
you had in childhood
when you were sisters
is one of the great joys
of growing up.

GOLDIE HAWN, B.1945,
FROM "A LOTUS GROWS IN THE MUD"

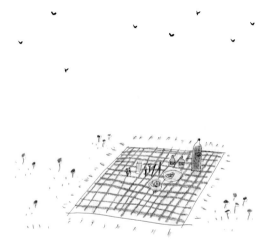

Sophisticated sisters,
long apart,
can turn into giggly schoolgirls
over just one cup of coffee.

PAM BROWN, B.1928

She is laughter,

even on the cloudy days of life;

nothing bothers her or saddens her

...She is the side of me that God left out.

Her funny stories...

her ability to interest herself

in a hundred and one people...

her talent for quick and warm friendships,

her philosophy of silver linings...

LILLIAN GISH (1893–1993)

Chance made us sister

earts made us friends.

AUTHOR UNKNOWN

Though we work together
and live three blocks apart,
     we must speak at least
twice a day on the phone.

My boyfriend and her husband
just don't get it.
We do – we're sisters.

STEPHANIE ABBAJAY

THE APPLAUSE OF A SISTER
MEANS FAR MORE
THAN THAT OF ANY CROWD.
FOR THEY SEE YOUR ACHIEVEMENT.
SHE SEES ALL
THAT LED UP TO IT.

PAM BROWN, B.1928

My sister is…

my memory – she brings back to life

all our happy childhood days,

she makes me feel secure.

MARY, AGE 76

When you're growing up, a sister
can be a ready-made playmate;
as a teenager, you've got a live-in counsellor,
as a mother,
you've got a willing babysitter,
in old age, you've got someone
who doesn't get bored by all your stories
of the "good old days".

JANE DOWDESWELL, FROM "SISTERS ON SISTERS"

Sheyna... was an unusual person,
and for me she was a shining example,
my dearest friend and my mentor.
Even late in life when we were both
grown women, grandmothers in fact,
Sheyna was the one person
whose praise and approval...
– meant most to me.

GOLDA MEIR (1898–1978), FROM "MY LIFE"

She was the refug

all the storms of my life....

BENJAMIN DISRAELI (1804–1881)

I cannot see my relationships with
my sisters ever dying or being forgotten.
No matter where I am. I can't explain it,
but that is where I have come to.
Even though we live far apart
there is something
extraordinarily strong between us.

FIONA BURKE,
FROM "SISTERS: LOVE AND CONFLICT
WITHIN THE LIFELONG BOND"

...she is t

ly sister I could ever want.

CRICKET HARDIN VAUTHIER,
FROM "ANIMAL CRACKER DRESSES"

It wouldn't have been like my sister
to throw her arms around me the day
our mother died... she offered me
the one promise she
could wholeheartedly make.
"I'm the only one now who remembers
the day of your birth," she told me.
"No matter what,
I will always be your sister."

JOYCE MAYNARD, ABOUT HER SISTER RONA

Often, in old age,
they become each other's chosen
and most happy companions.
In addition
to their shared memories of childhood

they share memories of the same home,
and the same small prejudices
about housekeeping that carry the echoes
of their mother's voice.

MARGARET MEAD (1901–1978),
FROM "BLACKBERRY WINTER"

We shared. Parents. Home. Pets.
Celebrations. Catastrophes. Secrets.
And the threads of our experience
became so interwoven
that we are linked.
I can never be utterly lonely,
knowing you share the planet.

PAM BROWN, B.1928

Sisters. Yes, we're just sisters.
Our story is not heroic,
not even memorable....
I remember quiet days –
with no great dramas,
no great acts of sisterly devotion.
But when I need support
I sense you quietly by me.
I always will.

HELEN THOMSON

Friends com

...riends go. Sisters are forever.

PAM BROWN, B.1928

Helen Exley runs her own publishing company which sells giftbooks in more than seventy countries. Helen fell in love with Joanna Kidney's happy, bright pictures and knew immediately they had the feel she was looking for. She asked Joanna to work on *smile, friend, happy day!, love* and *hope! dream!* We have now published eleven more books in this series, which are selling in 27 languages.

Joanna Kidney lives in County Wicklow in Ireland. She juggles her time between working on cards, books illustrations, and her own art for shows and exhibitions, and looking after her baby boy. Her whole range of greeting cards, *Joanna's Pearlies* – some of which appear in this book – won the prestigious Henries oscar for 'best fun or graphic range'.